5 Proven Methods For Making $1,000+ Per Month With Websites

By Chris Guthrie

http://ChrisGuthrieBooks.com

5 Proven Methods For Making $1,000+ Per Month With Websites
Copyright © 2014 Chris Guthrie All Rights Reserved

Disclaimer and Terms of Use

The author and publisher of this book and the accompanying materials have used their best efforts in preparing this book. The author and publisher make no representation or warranties with respect to the accuracy, applicability, fitness, or completeness of the contents of this book. The information contained in this book is strictly for informational purposes. Therefore, if you wish to apply ideas contained in this book, you are taking full responsibility for your actions.

Every effort has been made to accurately represent this book and it's potential. Even though this industry is one of the few where one can write their own check in terms of earnings, there is no guarantee that you will earn any money using the techniques and ideas in these materials. Examples in these materials are not to be interpreted as a promise or guarantee of earnings. Earning potential is entirely dependent on the person using our book, ideas, and techniques. We do not purport this as a "get rich scheme." Any claims made of actual earnings or examples of actual results can be verified upon request. Your level of success in attaining the results claimed in our materials depends on the time you devote to the knowledge and various skills. Since these factors differ according to individuals, we cannot guarantee your success or income level. Nor are we responsible for any of your actions

Materials in our product and our website may contain information that includes or is based upon forward-looking statements within the meaning of the securities litigation reform act of 1995. Forward-looking statements give our expectations or forecasts of future events. You can identify these statements by the fact that they do not relate strictly to historical or current facts. They use words such as "anticipate," "estimate," "expect," "project," "intend," "plan," "believe," and other words and terms of similar meaning in connection with a description of potential earnings or financial performance.

Any and all forward-looking statements here or on any of our sales material are intended to express our opinion of earnings potential. Many factors will be important in determining your actual results and no guarantees are made that you will achieve results similar to ours or anybody else's, in fact no guarantees are made that you will achieve any results from our ideas and techniques in our material.

The author and publisher disclaim any warranties (express or implied), merchantability, or fitness for any particular purpose. The author and publisher shall in no event be held liable to any party for any direct, indirect, punitive, special, incidental, or other consequential damages arising directly or indirectly from any use of this material, which is provided "as is" and without warranties.

As always, the advice of a competent legal, tax, accounting, or other professional should be sought.

The author and publisher do not warrant the performance, effectiveness, or applicability of any sites listed or linked to in this book.

All links are for information purposes only and are not warranted for content, accuracy, or any other implied or explicit purpose.

Table of Contents

Table of Contents

Your Free Bonus

Introduction to Making $1,000 a Month from Websites

Making $1,000+ per Month with a Website: Open Case Study

#1 How To Make Money with Niche Websites

#2 How To Make Money with Authority Websites

#3 How To Make Money with E-commerce Websites

#4 How To Make Money with Membership Websites

#5 How To Make Money with Review Websites

Conclusion

Excerpt from "How to Make Money as an Amazon Associate"

More Books by Chris Guthrie

Your Free Bonus

In addition to access to the over 2 hours of conversations with successful website entrepreneurs, I've also created a free 10-day course on how to make money with websites.

Access all the recordings from this book here (direct individual links are mentioned later in the book):

http://chrisguthriebooks.com/websites-book-recordings

I've been making money from websites full-time for more than half a decade, so you can bet I've made a lot of mistakes along the way. I created a free 10-day course to help you get started as quickly as possible, while simultaneously avoiding the common mistakes I made when I was first starting out.

http://chrisguthriebooks.com/free-10-day/

Enjoy these free bonuses, and I'm excited for you to read this book and continue on to build your own successful and profitable website.

Introduction to Making $1,000 a Month from Websites

Hello, my name is Chris Guthrie, and from the day I earned my first money from an Adsense click way back in 2005, I've been passionate about growing my online income. In 2009, after overcoming failures and building an increasing online income, I made the leap to full time internet entrepreneur, and I never looked back. You're reading this book because perhaps your goal is to do the same thing – build an online business so you can leave your day job. Or maybe you're just looking to earn some extra income online to help pay the bills. Regardless of why you're here, I'm glad you found this book, and I'm excited to share with you these 5 ways to earn at least $1,000 per month or more with websites. My goal is to help shorten your learning curve and provide you with some actionable advice to start or grow your internet income.

I'm very experienced in a lot of the methods I'll be sharing with you in this book and supplemental material, but this book is different in that I've interviewed experts in their fields and shared their thoughts with you in this book. In addition to reading this book, I encourage you to download the bonus audio recordings and listen to those as well to help provide you with actionable advice on how you can start or grow your own website.

Making $1,000+ per Month with a Website: Open Case Study

The information in this book on making money online with websites is more than enough to get you going on your own projects. However, sometimes it is nice to see step by step a website being built from the ground up.

This is exactly what I'm doing on my blog, EntrepreneurBoost.com.

I share everything from start to finish, along with the URL of the website I'm building. You can see my income, what I tried during the month to grow the website, along with what did and didn't work for me.

The techniques I share in the case study are helpful to anyone trying to get a website earning up to $1,000 a month.

You can follow my free case study on my blog here:

http://entrepreneurboost.com/1kblogmonth1/

#1 How To Make Money with Niche Websites

I've been making money with websites since 2005, and during the past several years, I've made money from both (large) authority websites, as well as (small) niche websites. Most of my focus is on building or acquiring larger authority style websites these days, but that isn't because you can't make money with niche websites. On the contrary, niche websites are still a viable method for generating relatively passive income. Now before I get ahead of myself, you might be wondering – **What is a niche website?** A niche website is typically a smaller website focused on a very narrow topic. For example, instead of writing about farming, a niche website would be focused only on worm farming. The work required to build a niche website requires you to research a niche, create the website, write content, monetize that content with ads, and then generate traffic from Google.

To provide an even more in-depth look at niche websites, I've interviewed one of my long time friends and niche website expert, Spencer Haws. Spencer currently generates thousands of dollars per month from Google Adsense and other programs from a portfolio of niche websites.

Bonus Audio Interview: Spencer Haws – How to Build a Portfolio of Passive Income Earning Niche Websites

Listen Here: http://chrisguthriebooks.com/spencer-haws-bonus

I've highlighted the most important concepts from this interview in this book if you'd prefer to read on without stopping to listen to the interview.

How To Research a Niche:

Niche research is the most important step in the process of building a niche website, and where you can help improve your chances at profitable success or guarantee you'll fail. So how do you research a niche? Well there are a variety of free and premium tools that can help you. When I first started out, I used the free Google Adwords Keyword Planner, which allows you to input a keyword and see how many times it is searched each month. In the bonus interview with Spencer, he shared one of his niche websites, BestSurvivalKnifeGuide.com, and to continue with his example, this is the data on the Google Adwords Keyword Planner that shows up for his niche website case study primary keyword, "best survival knife."

Google Adwords Keyword Planner

▼ Get search volume for a list of keywords or group them into ad groups

Option 1: Enter keywords

best survival knife|

Option 2: Upload file

[Choose File] No file chosen
Supported files and formats

Targeting [?]

United States

Google

Negative keywords

Date range [?]

Show avg. monthly searches for: Last 12 months

[Get search volume]

After you hit search, you'll see exactly how many people search that phrase each and every month:

After you've looked up the keyword and determined it has a sufficient amount of searches per month (a few thousand or more is ideal), it's then time to look at the competition on Google. The goal is to pick a niche that has very little competition, and you can determine the competition by using browser add-ons like **SEOQuake** for Firefox or Google Chrome, and **Mozbar** for Firefox or Google Chrome. These extensions help show you precisely how many links are pointing at the websites ranking in the top 10 in Google for that keyword.

Once you install the extensions on your browser, you can search for your target keyword in Google, and SEOQuake and Mozbar will display information below each result. This information will include Page Rank, Page Authority, Domain Authority, and Backlinks.

Another factor is to actually visit each page and look at the keyword that individual website is targeting. You can get an idea of what keyword they are trying to rank for by seeing what words they have in common from their title, first paragraph and headers. If they only have "survival knife", but not "best survival knife", then that means their page is optimized just for "survival knife".

If in this example they're targeting only "survival knife," but they're ranking for "best survival knife," that's another good indicator that there isn't a lot of competition for that keyword. If there was a lot of competition, then most – if not all – of the pages would be targeting "best survival knife" as a keyword.

So this can be a manual process of researching these websites if you want to use the free tools – that's how I got my  start. However, Spencer created a premium tool called *LongTailPro* that can save you a lot of time. I've been using *LongTailPro* for keyword research for over a year, and the tool helps to automate the process of finding valuable keywords, as well as determining how competitive a keyword is. Spencer is offering a **30% discount** to readers of this book, which is accessible here:

http://chrisguthriebooks.com/longtailprodiscount

Also on that page you can access a free trial of *Long Tail Pro*. I don't want you to think that you have to spend money to get started (I didn't at first either). The only reason why I tell you about these premium tools is because they'll save you time.

How To Create the Website

Many people that build niche websites (or authority websites for that matter) use free software called Wordpress. Most hosting providers, such as HostGator (who I use), allow you to install Wordpress from within your hosting control panel with a few clicks of a button. If you need website hosting, use the **kindlechris** coupon at checkout for **25% off hosting** when buying from HostGator.com. You can then use a wide variety of free and paid Wordpress plugins or themes to customize the look and functionality of your website. Both Spencer and I created a premium Wordpress theme specifically for niche websites that you can purchase at NicheWebsiteTheme.com, but again, if you're just starting out and want to spend as little money as possible, you can always use a free theme. The only thing you really need is a domain name (ideally the domain name is related to your keyword) and web hosting to host your website.

How To Write the Content

Niche research and content writing go hand in hand. The niche research that you initially conduct for your website should also double as a preliminary look into what kind of content you should write for your website. When you're analyzing your competition, you can get a sense of what type of articles and content they've created for their website. One of the tools I use is SEMRush.com to determine what keywords my competitors are ranking for, along with which pages are ranking. This helps me build a quick list of content that I can create for my competing website. The free tool only allows you to see a smaller subset of the results, but it does show the highest traffic keywords, which you can use to direct your focus at initially in your website building process.

Actually, writing the content is another step in the process, and where many people will start to outsource the process. Writing a lot of content can be very time consuming, so here are some of the best places to hire others to write the content for you:

TextBroker.com, Elance.com, Odesk.com, HireWriters.com

TextBroker allows you to set the quality you're looking for and briefly explain what the article should cover. I've personally used TextBroker for several different websites and have been pleased with the results. You can also consider hiring on a full time virtual assistant to write content for your websites. This is another strategy that my interviewee and I have used in the past.

How To Monetize the Website

There are a variety of methods for making money with niche websites, but the most common are contextual advertising and affiliate marketing. Google Adsense is a contextual advertising solution that allows you to insert advertising blocks in varying sizes that display links to advertisers that are automatically related to the content displaying on your website. I've personally made tens of thousands of dollars from Google's Adsense program, and Spencer has made even more with Adsense. The best method for making money with Google Adsense is to insert advertisements directly into the content area of your website, ideally near the beginning and end of an article. Your website visitors will focus most of their attention on the content area of an article, which is precisely why you should expect to earn the most money possible by placing a Google Adsense block at the beginning of your content, as well as the end of your content, to maximize your click through rate.

Amazon Associates is an affiliate marketing program that provides a commission for the sale of any products that a website refers to Amazon.com. This strategy is the primary monetization method Spencer is using on his BestSurvivalKnifeGuide.com website that we discussed in the interview. If you plan on making money with Amazon's affiliate program, it's crucial to be sure that the niche website you're building fits that strategy. In the example website Spencer shared, it's very clear that Amazon is the best choice, because the types of visitors that he'll get from

Google are people looking for the best survival knife. Once these people find the best survival knife, they're probably very interested in buying it as well. So it's important to include a variety of text affiliate links in the content you write linking to various products related to your niche. Additionally, when you post images, you can link to products using your affiliate link that way as well. The number one reason people fail to make money with Amazon's affiliate program is because they try and force the strategy where it doesn't work.

It takes a while to go to Amazon.com, find a product you want to promote, create the affiliate link, and then copy that code into your website. I've built a tool that allows you to insert Amazon affiliate links from within your WordPress powered website so you don't have to go to Amazon to do it. You can check that tool out at EasyAzon.com.

When it comes to making money with Amazon's affiliate program, I've earned over **$100,000+ in commissions**, so if you're really interested in making money with Amazon, check out my other Kindle book all about it: http://ChrisGuthrieBooks.com/Amazon.

While Spencer and I have both had success with niche sites focused on physical products and using Amazon Affiliates, you can have success simply through advertising your niche site. Another option is to use a site such as clickbank.com to find affiliations for non-physical items. You can simply visit the site, type in the topic of your niche, and find affiliate programs to sign up for and promote on your site.

Book Update: Spencer isn't using that domain anymore. Read this blog post to find out why: http://www.nichepursuits.com/survival-knife-project-update-making-a-comback-from-negative-seo/ The advice shared earlier in the book is still applicable, but this has more to do with the fact that someone attacked Spencer's public case study.

How To Generate Traffic to the Website

Niche websites generate most of their traffic by ranking for various keywords in Google. So how do you rank for keywords in Google? Well, the primary factor for ranking websites is the number and quality of backlinks that are pointed at your website. Other major factors include content relevancy (you can't rank for best survival knife if your website is about baby cribs), quality of content (don't pay as little as possible if you're outsourcing content creation), and quantity of content (the more relevant content on your website the better). So if you're building a niche website about a specific topic, it's a great strategy to write a wide range of articles related to a variety of different keywords. But it doesn't matter if you write a lot of content if you don't market that content, which is precisely what building links is all about.

Building links for niche websites isn't very difficult, but it can be monotonous, which is why this activity is typically outsourced just like content creation. Over time, the effectiveness of using the same link building tactics can change, and strategies that used to work may stop working or require tweaking. The reason why these link building tactics change is because Google is always changing their algorithm, so if you're building niche websites, you need to also commit to continue learning about search engine optimization and link building tactics as well.

One of the best resources for staying up-to-date on Google algorithm changes is Moz's Google Algorithm Change History:

http://moz.com/google-algorithm-change

Some of the easiest and effective strategies for link building include: writing comments on blogs related to your niche and getting a link back to your website; article marketing where you write real articles and put them on article directories (Ezinearticles.com, Goarticles.com, Squidoo.com, HubPages.com); web directories where you can list your website in their directories (abc-directory.com, freeprwebdirectory.com, medranks.com, directory.ac, sitepromotiondirectory.com – there are a lot of these available); getting links from private blog networks (PBN's); and contacting individual site owners by email to try and get added to their resource pages.

The good thing about niche sites is that you typically don't need an extreme amount of links to rank in Google. You simply need to beat out your competitors. Once you start ranking higher in Google, more people will see your site, and you will begin to start getting natural links. You simply have to put in the work with link building at the beginning in order to start to rise up the ranks in Google.

Being in the top three spots is typically where the most money is.

If your site is starting to bring in a lot of money, you can even begin to consider advertising to get traffic. Before you go and pay for Facebook ads or Google Adwords, you should figure out how much money you are making per visitor. You can use Google Analytics to figure out how many visitors your website is getting. Once you have your profit per visitor figured out, you can compare that to how much it would cost you to run ads. If your profit per visitor is greater than your cost per visitor using ads, then you should give advertising a try.

An example of all this is, if on average, you make $1,000 per month from your niche site, and are getting 4,000 visitors a month, then you are making $0.25 per visitor. Then you test out a Facebook ad campaign with $50, and find out that you received 500 visitors from that campaign. This means it cost you $0.10 per customer. This means that for every customer you received from the Facebook campaign was $0.15 of profit. This means you can ramp up the advertising to make even more money.

#2 How To Make Money with Authority Websites

Authority websites are something that I have a lot of experience with. They have made up a very large amount of my online income, one in particular that I will get into later in the book, since it is an authority site and a review site. For looking at authority sites however, I talked with Peter Armstrong, who created and runs babynamegenie.com. Before I talk about how to build and monetize authority sites, I want to share more on what exactly an authority site is.

An authority site is similar to a niche website, in that you want to focus on one specific topic. Authority websites are typically on broader topics than niche websites. Referring to my previous example from niche websites, an authority site could be about farming, while the niche website would only be about worm farming. However, for authority sites, your goal is to build out a website that ends up being the authority on that topic. As for Peter, that topic was baby names. Since authority sites are on broader topics than niche sites, they take longer to build out and monetize. But in my experience, the longer time ends up being a bigger payoff. As for Peter and his website, he has seen this bigger payout in the form of becoming a "premium ad space" website, which I will explain soon.

Bonus Audio Interview: Peter Armstrong – How to Build a Successful Authority Website.

Listen Here: http://chrisguthriebooks.com/peter-armstrong-bonus

I've highlighted the biggest points from Peter's interview if you would rather keep reading:

How To Decide on a Topic for Your Authority Site

There are a couple paths you can take for coming up with your authority site idea. One that I have used is to follow new trends and technologies coming out. I was able to create a netbook review website early on and became an authority in that niche. On top of that, the market research talked about for niche websites is always a helpful tool to gauge the size and popularity of topics. Peter had a different approach, in that he had a problem that he couldn't find a good answer too.

Peter was expecting a child and was trying to decide on a name. When looking for resources online, he realized there weren't any that solved his problem. Being inspired by a team name generator he came across online, he was inspired to create a similar website, but for baby names.

This method of realizing a problem you have that there isn't a good solution for is a great way to come up with ideas for authority sites. Even if you don't have the solution on hand for the problem, you can do some research and come up with a better solution than what is out there. All you need is to be slightly better than what is already available and build the site from there.

Getting Started on an Authority Site

This is exactly what Peter did. Working 5-10 hours a week on his project, he developed a baby name generator. While Peter is skilled at web developing and could create this on his own, those of us that don't know how to do something like that can easily outsource it on sites such as Elance.com or Odesk.com.

After developing your authority site and getting your main content on there, you can test it quickly and cheaply like Peter did to get validation of his idea. Peter went into forums and start interacting with people interested in baby names.

This worked for Peter because he didn't push his site. He simply interacted with people, provided value to them, and added in his website in his signature. People began visiting and sharing his site. This shows the importance of quality content for authority sites. Since you are not in a niche that will be smaller and easier to rank in Google, you need people to be interested in and sharing your content.

An early way to tell if your content is sharable is to do exactly what Peter did. Find out where people you think would be interested in your topic are hanging out online and go and engage with them. Don't push your site, but make sure a link is available if people find your interactions valuable and want to get more value from you.

Making Money with Authority Sites

The great thing about authority sites is that they offer multiple ways to make money. For Peter, it was through advertising. For my netbooks site, it was with Amazon affiliate links. Since you are considered an authority on the topic, you can then create information products or write eBooks on the subject. Since creating and selling products and eBooks is more difficult, we will focus on Peter's method of advertising (since I discuss the netbook review site later on).

One mistake to avoid for beginners that Peter mentions in my interview with him, and that I completely agree about, is that you can't be afraid to put advertisements on your website. If you take a minute to look at the sites that you most often go to, there are advertisements on them. All of the biggest and most trustworthy websites have some sort of advertisements on them, so you shouldn't be afraid to put them on yours.

The easiest way to start with ads for your site is with Google AdSense. The easiest way to add AdSense to your site is with the Quick Sense WP plugin. It allows you to put up the ads in minutes and place them exactly where you want. When it comes to putting ads on your site, Peter and I both recommend 3 ad units (images) and 2 link ads. In this post from my website, you can see steps on how to maximize your Adsense earnings.

While AdSense is a good start and you can make over $1,000 a month using AdSense, you get higher advertising money if your website is considered "premium ad space." By premium ad space, this means that your website attracts a lot of visitors all from a specific demographic or one important trait. Since companies want to advertise to their ideal market, they are willing to pay more if they can advertise on websites where that ideal market goes. This is called an aggregate business model.

For Peter and Baby Name Genie, his demographic was people expecting to have a child. For companies that sell baby products, what better website is there to advertise on? This is how Peter utilized his authority in the baby naming industry to boost his advertising revenue well into the thousands. So while authority sites do take longer to build out that niche sites, they end up having a bigger payout when it comes to advertising.

Should You Use Advertisements to Get More Visitors?

Getting a lot of visitors is important for any website, but it is extremely important when your revenue is based off of ad impressions (how many times an ad is seen by a visitor). One tempting thing to try out is to advertise to get people onto your site. Some of the more popular forms of this are [Facebook Ads](#) and [Google AdWords](#). While this can work very well for your website, you should do some math that Peter recommended to make sure.

Peter found out how much profit he makes per visitor, and the average percentage of return visitors for his website. You can use Google Analytics to figure out your monthly and returning visitors. Peter used this number to decide if buying traffic via ads would cost more or less than his profit per visitor. For him, he would be losing money on the advertisements. While advertising didn't work for Peter, it may work for another authority site, so I recommend doing the quick math to figure it out.

Getting More Visitors to an Authority Site

Along with advertising, there are a number of ways to get people to your authority website. One of the ways is exactly the same as with niche websites. Find out long tail keywords that people are searching for on Google, write articles for those keywords, and then focus on getting high quality links back to your site.

Fortunately for authority sites that are publishing high quality content, this offers multiple avenues for getting traffic. One of the ways is that high quality content gets talked about on the internet. Other blogs that like your content will link to it, which will move you up in Google. Also, with high quality content, users want to share it with their friends and family.

For Peter, one extremely sharable part of his website was his baby name poll, which allows users to put up multiple baby names and get people to vote on them. This ended up being one of the most shared aspects of Peter's site. The key to come up with something like that is to focus on interactive and fun things for your site.

#3 How To Make Money with E-commerce Websites

An e-commerce site is a website that sells physical goods. Unlike selling through affiliates, which I talked about before, e-commerce sites sell directly from their own site. While this is more work and responsibility for this type of website (shipping, returns, stock levels, etc.), the margins are much higher. There are different strategies you can use to run an e-commerce store. You can create your own product, or you can buy existing products and sell them. You can house your inventory, or you can drop ship your inventory, which means the supplier is the one who ships it to the consumer. All have their advantages and disadvantages.

I've been selling physical products on Amazon, but at the time of publishing, I have less experience with general e-commerce strategies than I do the other types of websites in this book. However, I interviewed Dan Andrews about e-commerce. Dan is an expert in the different variations of e-commerce and makes a lot of money doing it.

Bonus Audio Interview: Dan Andrews – Using E-commerce to Make Thousands of Dollars a Month

Listen Here: http://chrisguthriebooks.com/dan-andrews-bonus

I've cover the main points of the interview below, so you can continue reading, if you prefer:

What Are Some Example E-commerce Websites Dan Runs

In the interview, Dan shared a few of his e-commerce websites, including:

ModernCatDesigns.com (cat furniture store), and one of his newer e-commerce stores is ThePortableBarCompany.com (just as it sounds - a portable bar store).

What Software Can You Use to Run E-commerce Websites

In Dan's case, he's been building and managing e-commerce websites for several years, so he has experience with the following e-commerce software platforms: Shopify, BigCommerce, Drupal and WooCommerce. All of his e-commerce stores are now built on WooCommerce, which is a solution for Wordpress powered websites. Ultimately, you want to focus on using only one e-commerce platform so that if you create new websites, you can leverage your existing knowledge of that platform.

How To Come Up with E-commerce Ideas

In a story that should sound familiar, the best advice for generating ideas is to look for pain points in your own life that you can solve with a product that you create and sell for others. In this case, Dan's business partner is a cat lover, and while shopping for cat furniture, noticed that everything on the market was ugly. So they set out to create better-looking cat furniture, which he admits later, wasn't the best problem that needed to be solved – but it was a start. In another instance, his business partner was a valet parker, and he understood the problems that could be solved in that profession, so they created a whole line of products for valet parking. This is a recurring theme that I've seen repeated both in the experts I interviewed for this book, as well as other entrepreneur friends I've been in contact with. Beyond the advice Dan shared in the interview, I think we can again come back to performing market research using the same keyword research tools I've mentioned several times before (Google Adwords Keyword Planner, Long Tail Pro, etc). Doing this research can help to gauge how much interest there is in a product or product line, that you could then develop using Dan's strategy of creating something worthy and building a narrative and community around.

How To Get a Prototype Product Created

One of the strategies Dan uses with his e-commerce business is to generate a virtual prototype of a product he wants to build using a program called <u>SolidWorks</u>. Next he'll shop it around to the various suppliers in China and get an actual product made. Then he takes photos of the product and starts to drive traffic to the page. Dan's a big believer in using a phone number as a way to sell products, as well as connect with customers for products early in development. This strategy works much better in the business-to-business space though, where often the customers have more incentive to care about the end product they purchase, as they'll be using it in their business. Dan's even tested the market by selling products that weren't created yet by simply posting a picture of the prototype, driving traffic, and then returning the money to the customers once they've purchased, simply to confirm there was demand.

How To Succeed as an E-commerce Store in an Amazon World

With billions and billions of dollars in annual sales, Amazon is absolutely massive in the e-commerce space, so as a reader contemplating this method for earning money online, you might be wondering how it's possible to succeed against Amazon at all. Dan's advice is that one effective method of competing is by cultivating that personal relationship with the customer, which again is why he's such a strong believer in posting his phone number for customers to call. He further added that it's the wrong approach to have a clever SEO strategy or a clever Pay Per Click advertising strategy, and then think you can rank for a lot of terms in Google with an e-commerce store. His best advice is to have a product that people are interested in talking about, and if you can bring that to the marketplace, you're going to be able to build an audience and consistently sell into that audience. As a real life example, he compared his own ModernCatDesigns.com cat furniture store to another store started at around the same time called hauspanther.com. With hauspanther, the creator of the site has tens of thousands of email subscribers, and she was able to cultivate a community around people that care about cat furniture. In comparison, now three years later, she is in a much better position to have a successful line of cat furniture products than Dan does as a producer of cat furniture trying to rank their products in Google.

Just because you are focusing on quality relationships with customers and building an actual brand, that doesn't mean you should ignore advertising as a means to grow your business. Typically, e-commerce stores will have a higher profit per visitor, because the visitors are actually purchasing something from the site. This means that you have a better chance of pulling a profit using advertising.

Deciding To Drop Ship or Create the Products Yourself

Drop shipping is a strategy that can work in e-commerce, but Dan says the good opportunities won't be found on WorldWideBrands.com (a drop shipping directory website). You have to identify your niches and build a relationship with the people you're going to be partnering with. Drop shipping can work for someone like hauspanther.com that's built an audience and a narrative around cat furniture products. The problem is that if you want the products to sell themselves on the merits of the product, drop shipping isn't the way to go - you've got to develop your own products, and that's the strategy Dan's focused on and seen the most success with. The profit is much better when you're manufacturing yourself, and you have a differentiation for which you can charge for. Dan's background is industrial design, so without that he may have taken a different approach instead of manufacturing his own products. Using his example, ThePortableBarCompany.com, they found that there were other portable bars on the market that were selling really well (which is always a good sign), but the competitors weren't addressing the market with higher end portable bars. So they decided to create higher end portable bars and begin selling those. If you want to go the manufacturing route, one of the best websites to get started is Alibaba.com.

Selling Goods Means Customer Service

One of the responsibilities that come with building out an e-commerce site is that you now need to deal with customer service. This includes anything from returns, to complaints, to items being out of order. Good customer service is one of the best ways to stand out from your competition. It is less expensive to keep existing customers, than it is to go out and find new ones. This means that you should be treating your existing customers as good as possible. They will end up either returning to buy more from you again or recommending you to others. Great customer service is often an overlooked way to grow your business.

Update: I started selling physical products on Amazon.com. You can read about my first month selling, and you'll also be able to see updated links to future reports via this page as well:

http://entrepreneurboost.com/first-30-amazon/

#4 How To Make Money with Membership Websites

Membership sites are similar to niche and authority sites in that they are websites based around one topic, and they produce content on that topic. However, membership sites differ in how they are monetized. Membership sites are websites that have a section that is strictly members only, and you have to pay to get access to this section. To get even greater detail on membership sites, I interviewed <u>Stu McLaren</u>.

Stu is the creator of <u>WishList Products</u>, a software that can convert any website into a membership site. This software allows you to create content behind a pay wall and charge people for access to it. This is a great way to monetize content you are putting on your website, and this content can come in different forms, which shapes the business style of your membership website. There are three main types of membership sites that Stu talked about in the interview, and before I get into what they are and how to set them up, I just want to remind you that you can get the full interview from Stu in the free bonus.

Bonus Audio Interview: Stu McLaren – Generating Thousands of Dollars with Membership Sites.

Listen Here: http://chrisguthriebooks.com/stu-mclaren-bonus

Once again, the main points are below if you prefer to keep reading:

The 3 Types of Membership Sites

Protected Download Area

The first type of membership site that Stu talked about, and the one that I personally use, is a protected download area. This is a distinct webpage that is protected by a pay wall that holds the download link of your products. These products can come in the forms of eBooks, videos, audiobooks, or one-time courses. This is perfect if you have an eBook you want to sell personally on your website, or if you have a course to teach. Users make a one-time payment to get access to this webpage, and the content on it.

You can take whatever topic your site is about and expand it into an eBook or videos series and put it behind a pay wall. You can even combine different forms of sharing this knowledge into one course. This is what I personally use for some of my websites that sell digital goods, like EasyAzon.com, for example. This is a relatively easy way to set up a website and get a product on the market to sell.

If you already have a website set up and simply want to package everything on it nicely into a course or eBook, you could simply send all the articles over to a freelance writer to put it all together. You can then get a design for the course or eBook cover for $5 from Fiverr.

Modular Course

The second style of membership site that Stu mentions is a modular training course. This is similar to the course style mentioned above, except that you continuously teach something new each month. This takes more work, but is great because you get a reoccurring revenue stream from this style of site, since you can charge members monthly fees.

The way that it works is members sign up to your site, and you have a new lesson for them every month, where you are either training them or teaching them something. This works great since it allows you to drip information to them over time and gives you a head start on creating content for the next month. I will discuss more about this style of website after covering the last style of membership site.

Publisher Membership

This website is similar to the modular course in that members pay a monthly fee to join your website. However, this isn't a website where there is a course involved that people follow along with. It is simply a pay wall in front of your regular content. The best example of this kind of site is online newspapers and magazines. You login into their sites to get access to the articles that aren't available publicly.

Examples of Membership Sites

While those are the three types of membership sites, they can truly come in many different forms and may include more than one type. In the interview, Stu named a few examples that you are welcome to check out. A few of them are Herbmentor.com, webartacademy.com, wp101.com, and cbiclubhouse.com.

These websites are a good illustration that you can create a membership websites on just about any topic. Herb Mentor is obviously about herbs, while CBI Clubhouse is focused purely on writing children's books (and has over 3,000 members).

How To Begin with a Membership Site

Like most of the other sites, membership sites can start either with market research or solving a problem you personally have in life. Once you realize that you can generate income from almost any topic (make sure to do market research like we talked about earlier), you start to see potential website ideas all the time. They can come from things you are passionate about, things that you are curious about, or problems that you have encountered. Again, if you don't think you're an expert when it comes to a certain niche, you are probably wrong. Stu quoted Desiderius Erasmus in the interview to make this point:

"In the land of the blind, the one-eyed man is king."

Next you should select how you want to structure your content, which informs your decision on what type of membership site to set up. If you want to sell something one time, then it's best to go with the protected pay wall. If you want to continuously teach people, then you can take advantage of the monthly membership of the modular course set up.

Once you have selected your membership site structure, you need to start creating content and the product. The protected download area is straightforward in that you create the product, then market your product and website as much as possible. There are numerous ways to market your website, such as Facebook Ads, ranking in Google, or creating social media accounts. You simply are trying to get as many people to your site and buying your product as possible with this model.

For the publisher membership and modular course, you need to be constantly preparing your sites and content. This is more work, but you do have the advantage of reoccurring payments from the members. If you are looking to get started, you need to produce both free content and paid content.

Free content is for anyone who visits the site, members and non-members. This free content is meant to peak curiosity and show that you are an authority on the subject. Stu talks of this free content as the "telling you what to do" content. By this he means that this content tells you what to do to reach your goal or solve your problem. For example, if you want to make money with websites, I could tell you to write content, find a way to monetize it, and get people to your website to buy your products or click on ads. This is simply just telling you what to do. The paid content, however, tells you how to do that. How to write content, how to monetize websites, and how to get people onto your website.

The "how to" content is what your paid content consists of. If you utilize a publishing membership, you simply need to post your new articles that are worth the membership fee. For newspapers and magazines, this is simply keeping the members as up-to-date as possible on a specific topic. For non-news sites, it could simply be really good content focused around one topic.

Paid content for modular courses can be split into three different groups: core content, primary content, and secondary content. Core content is content that is always available and is given to members once they join. The purpose of it is to get new members excited and give them a foundation to get started with.

The primary content is the main themes of the website. This is the lessons or solutions that you are giving to the customer. Your primary content is the reason people are paying to be on your site. This can be a mixture of teaching content, videos, Q&A's, and anything else you can think of. Stu recommends have 3 or 4 pieces of primary content for every month, and you can release one of them every week.

Stu mentioned that you are more than likely going to run into someone who complains that they aren't getting all the content all at once. One way that Stu explained solving this complaint is that content is dripped over a certain time period to give people time to learn the lessons and implement them.

Secondary content is extremely important as well. It is a better business plan to maintain users than it is to try and find new ones. Secondary content is made to keep existing users engaged and excited for next month's lessons. It can come in many forms. One idea is forum follow-ups, where you highlight the most popular threads in the forum for the week. You can also create announcements for next month, upcoming events, giveaways, or contests. The point is simply to keep people engaged between the primary content and excited to stay a member on your site for the following month.

Stu had a great tip on maintaining members in that you should be tracking your membership drop off over the years. This way, you can see patterns in people dropping off, such as there is a dip during the winter, but a spike in spring, followed by a dip at the start of summer. Once you recognize these patterns in dips, you can use the secondary content specifically to address those points in order to retain members. Maybe this is the time of year where you have the biggest give-away. Anything that gets members excited to stay on is key at these points.

How To Grow a Membership Site

Stu's tips for growing a membership site are similar to those we have talked about with the other websites, such as building an email list. Stu offered the advice to set up a homepage before you launch the site explaining what is coming and having an email opt-in. This way, when you do launch the site, you can have momentum from day one. You can also use paid traffic with advertising, along with targeting your free content to long tail keywords, to try to get people on the site from Google. It is very similar to marketing the other types of websites mentioned earlier in the book.

What Is Needed to Start

Although building out a modular membership site seems like more work than the other styles, it doesn't take much to get going. Stu recommended writing your free content, your core content, and 3-4 pieces of primary and secondary content. With this alone, you are ready to launch your website. This way you have a month to come up with next month's modular, consisting of 3-4 pieces of primary and secondary content, which allows you plenty of time.

#5 How To Make Money with Review Websites

The last website style that I will teach you is a review site. This is the style of website I personally used in part to help make over $100,000 with Amazon Affiliates commission and ended up selling the site for six figures. The site was netbookreviews.com. This review site is similar to the niche and authority sites I talk about earlier. While I did pick out a niche, it was more general than just one keyword. And while it was an authority site, it was focused purely on reviewing netbooks. The reason I focused primarily on netbook reviews is because if someone types into Google "netbook reviews," or "[brand name] review," they are most likely thinking of purchasing a netbook. I was targeting much more qualified traffic than just a general authority site on netbooks when it comes to trying to get them over to Amazon to buy something. The point of a review site is to target people who are looking to buy something, provide them valuable information on what they are looking to buy, and then send them over to Amazon.

Bonus Audio Interview: My Interview – Six Figure Amazon Review Website

Listen Here: http://chrisguthriebooks.com/chris-guthrie-bonus

The highlights are below:

How To Create a Review Site

As you can guess, coming up with a review site is similar to coming up with the other websites we have talked about. However, for a review site, you want to specifically focus on physical products so you can be an affiliate for Amazon. I chose my topic, netbooks, because I saw them as something new on the scene that would pick up in popularity, because they are a lighter version of a laptop. Following any niche and trying to find and stay on top of trends is a great way to build a site, because you will start a step ahead of everyone.

Since you work on commission with Amazon, the higher the price of the product, the more you get for your sale. You have to consider how many sales you can send to Amazon though. You can probably make more sales with a $100 product than with a $5,000 product, but the commission will be greater for the latter. That is research that you will have to look at on each specific product, price versus number of sales.

One good thing about a review site is that you can sell products of multiple price ranges. For example, with netbooks, they varied in price. You can also sell cheaper accessories on your review site as well. However, you don't need to worry about that to begin with, since Amazon will be trying to sell the customer accessories, and if you send someone to Amazon, you get a commission on everything they purchase on Amazon within 24 hours of clicking your link.

With all of the websites I have built in my career, review sites have been the best when it comes to being an

Amazon Affiliate. You'll want to make sure to grab EasyAzon (there's a free version and paid version) as well to help you monetize and create your site easier.

Growing a Review Site

When it comes to a review site, it is extremely helpful to be at the top of Google for your main topic, such as netbook reviews, along with specific brand reviews. Like I mentioned at the start of the book, you can use Google Keyword Planner or LongTail Pro to figure out some good long tail keywords for your site. You can also use SEMRush to see what reviews your competitors are ranking for. Then you can create better content than them, focused on those keywords.

The content you want to create on your site should differentiate you from the competition and create as much value for customers as possible. Some ideas that work well for review sites are creating videos to go with product review pages. These videos can be of your unpacking the product and reviewing it out loud, and eventually footage of you using it. One technique I used to differentiate myself was that I would search the web to find the PR department for brands of netbooks. I was able to contact them and get them to send me netbook products to review on video. This can work with any niche, since companies are looking for press and feedback on their products. You may not get to keep the product, but it'll get you something that competition may not have.

Another example that I and others use is comparing two products side-by-side in one article. If possible, you can compare multiple items in a product table. These are simple to create with the Wordpress plugin called WP Table Press (simply go to your Wordpress dashboard > plugins > search for plugins > type in "WP Table Press" > hit search > click install).

One strategy that I used to grow my site and get more visitors was to try to be the one who broke news on netbooks. I followed tech blogs, manufacturers, and anyone else who was talking about netbooks. Then as soon as I heard about something new coming out, I would post about it and try to get it featured on bigger blogs. One of my biggest boosts came from doing this during a lunch break at my "real" job and getting some great backlinks from the post that got on a few major tech sites.

Amazon Affiliate Tricks

When you start with Amazon, your commission rate starts at the lowest tier, which is 4%. The more products you sell, the higher your commission rate becomes.

Number of Products Shipped/Downloaded in a Given Month**	Volume-Based Advertising Rates for General Products
1–6	4.00%
7–30	6.00%
31–110	6.50%
111–320	7.00%
321–630	7.50%
631–1570	8.00%
1571–3130	8.25%
3131+	8.50%

One technique that I have used in the past is to make two review sites. One is a big ticket item worth a couple hundred to a few thousand dollars. The second one will focus on a cheaper item that I can move a lot of. This way, the cheaper item is helping my commission levels go up, which is helping me get a better commission on the big-ticket items.

Other strategies that I have used to increase my sales on review sites are to create a monthly best sellers list. This typically is a high converting piece of content. You should be building an email list, so you can send this monthly best sellers list out to them. Another thing that I would send out to my email lists were sales and promos during the holidays. I would massively increase my sales come the holidays.

Some more tips for Amazon affiliate sites are to create clickable links inside the content, make images affiliate linked back to Amazon, and use carousel banners over static banners. These are some of the tactics I used to increase my revenue. The goal is simply to try to get people onto Amazon.

You can increase traffic to your site the same way I described in the other website styles. Create content that ranks in Google, along with possibly using ads.

If you want to learn more about becoming an affiliate, I've written a book specifically on that, which you can see here:

http://chrisguthriebooks.com/Amazon

Conclusion

These 5 styles of websites discussed in this book are all great ways to make $1,000 a month or more. The best part about the 5 options is that they can all be used for pretty much any topic, and as you saw, the strategies often inter relate to each other. If you are interested in a subject, you can do keyword research to see if there is a market for it. If you have a problem that you aren't finding a good solution to, you can do market research and test ideas to find out if others are having the same problem.

You can then solve the problem in numerous ways. You can create a niche site about a very specific problem or create an authority site about a broader problem, and both can be used to make money with ad revenue and affiliate marketing. If your problem is more about a physical product, you can do what Dan did and create your own product. You can also teach lessons or sell eBooks through a membership site. If your problem is deciding between certain brands of products and no sources online are helpful, you can solve that problem by creating a review site.

There are problems that need to be solved all around you, and plenty of tools to find good keywords. You can be the one who capitalizes on them.

If you are interested in making money with websites, but don't want to put in the time to start from ground zero, you can always buy websites that are already making money. If you'd like to learn more about that, I have covered it in my book, "How to Buy and Sell Websites." You can check that out here:

The information in the book offers you plenty of plans and ideas for making $1,000 a month with a website. However, it is up to you to execute on a plan. For every reader of this book, I just ask that even if you don't pursue one of the options I shared in this book, at least pursue something. The only way you can succeed online is by simply starting somewhere. I failed my way to eventual success after trying bad idea after bad idea. Hopefully, the information I've shared in this book will cut your learning curve, and most importantly, give you the push you need to get started.

Don't Forget Your Free Bonus:

Don't forget to download the over two hours of interviews I conducted for the purpose of writing this introductory book. I've also included all of the tools mentioned in the book on this page as well. You can grab all that here:

http://chrisguthriebooks.com/websites-book-recordings

You can also start your free 10-day course on how to build a profitable website here. I created this course as a means to help others avoid making the same time consuming mistakes I did when I first got started. Take that free course here:

http://chrisguthriebooks.com/free-10-day/

Thank you again for buying and reading my book. I hope you move forward with building some type of website, whether it's a niche, authority, e-commerce, membership, or review website.

You made it to the end! If you enjoyed my book and would like to leave me a review, I'd really appreciate it. You can go direct to this link to write a review (and thanks in advance):

http://chrisguthriebooks.com/reviewbook4

Excerpt from "How to Make Money as an Amazon Associate"

Below I have included chapters two and three from my book "How to Make Money as an Amazon Associate". Since I covered being an Amazon Associate with the niche and review sites, I wanted to share with you some of the information that I put together for my book dedicated to the subject.

If you are interested in generating money from being an Amazon Associate and would like to learn the tactics I used to sell over $1 million worth of products, you can get the book here:

http://www.amazon.com/How-Make-Money-Amazon-Associate-ebook

Chapter 2. Why I Chose to Become an Amazon Affiliate

As a member of Amazon's affiliate program **you have the ability to recommend millions of products available for sale on Amazon.com** ranging from books to video games and everything in between and to receive a commission if someone purchases a product after clicking through your affiliate link. I'll discuss the various strategies to make money with Amazon's affiliate program later in this book, but **the vast product catalog allows you to choose from tens of thousands of niches to work in**.

Before using Amazon's affiliate program I made money by building popular websites that got tons of traffic and then I leveraged that traffic into income from ad clicks (i.e. Google Adsense). Unfortunately, this only ever made me a small income and certainly would not have allowed me to leave my day job.

An example of one of my ultimately flawed websites is **GamingVidz.com** – this was my first moderately successful website that at the height of its popularity (mid 2000's) managed to generate **only $500 per month** with Google Adsense despite garnering over **500,000 page views per month** (which is a relatively large amount of traffic). It was only after building GamingVidz.com and trying to make money from ads by sheer amounts of traffic that I realized there had to be a better way to make money. Sure there are websites around that make money from ads simply by focusing on getting a lot of traffic, but I recognized that another method could be to build websites that targeted niches where people were already looking to buy products. That way I could recommend products on my website that people were already looking to buy and earn a nice commission off each sale rather than hoping that the people that came to my website would click an ad on the sidebar so I could get 5 cents from Adsense. Don't get me wrong, I still make money from Adsense through various websites, but what appealed to me about Amazon was the chance at larger rewards for sales that I could refer.

I could go on sharing why recommending products on Amazon.com through their affiliate program is an effective monetization strategy but I'm sure you get my point by now so let's move onto the next section.

Chapter 3. What Makes a Successful Amazon Income Generating Website?

Alright, so I've already covered my background and explained why I chose to participate in Amazon's affiliate program but if you're a complete beginner I'd like to lay it all out so that you understand everything before we get into specific strategies for building websites.

3a. How I make money

I make money by building niche and authority style websites that target one or more keyword phrases that people search for in Google – the more someone searches for a phrase the better (but also the more competition there generally is). When people come to these websites they can read articles that I've written articles with affiliate links embedded within the content. When someone clicks those links they are taken to Amazon.com. After someone clicks one of my affiliate links as long as they buy an item in the next 24 hours I receive a commission for their purchase. I like to buy domain names that encompass the keyword phrase I'm targeting (or at least a portion of it). For example, one niche Amazon website I have is http://wirelesshdmi.net and I build that site to target the keyword phrase "wireless hdmi" which receives thousands of searches per month in Google's search engine. **That website has generated nearly $5,000 in commissions since I created it a few years ago.**

The goal behind each website is to build something that ranks in Google and other various search engines for the primary and secondary keywords that I'm targeting. In late September of 2012 Google updated their algorithm to reduce the bonus that EMD or exact match domains provided in regards to SEO. So the example "wireless hdmi" website that I've shown you using an exact match keyword domain name doesn't mean you need to go out and do the same thing. In fact, there is little reason to go out and spend a lot to buy a nice exact match keyword domain name if they aren't available to register because Google is treating all domains on the same playing field now. This just illustrates Google's continually changing algorithm and their desire to only allow the best sites to rise to the top search engine results.

Important Note: Google uses hundreds if not thousands of factors to influence search engine rankings and the way in which they rank websites continually changes. In the next section I'll discuss the strategy for more sites with lower quality or less sites that are higher quality.

3b. Google ranking basics – link building

One of the primary key factors that can influence rankings in Google is the number of links that point towards that website. **Crudely explained, links are basically counted as votes with the more votes a website has the more valuable it will appear in Google's eyes and the better search engine rankings it likely will have.** Now things are much more complex than this because each link isn't created equal in the eyes of Google. Paying $5 for someone to create 100 forum links pointed at your website from http://fiverr.com is not nearly as valuable as getting your website mentioned on http://engadget.com because you found out when a hot new product was recently listed on Amazon.com and you were the first tech site to report on it. I've used both of these tactics in the past with the latter being more effective, but obviously more time consuming.

In this book I intentionally want to steer clear of sharing any definitive strategies for link building precisely because of how fast Google updates their algorithm. Any strategy I share in this book could be effective for the next 24 hours or maybe the next 12 months from the time you've read it. In fact, less than 48 hours after I published this book I had to go back in and make some changes because of a Google algorithm update. With that said, there are some very simple guidelines you can follow if you want to limit your risk of Google deranking your websites:

The less effort you've expended to acquire a link the more likely it is to have less value over time in the eyes of Google

Going back to my earlier example clearly paying $5 for a pack of 100 forum links is less valuable than getting a link from one of the top tech blogs in the world because the forum links only cost me $5 and the link from http://engadget.com required me to closely follow a market and watch when highly anticipated products popped up for sale on Amazon.com and then send an email to their tips section in hopes that they'd pick it up.

Link building strategies also vary based on the type of website you want to build so the next thing I'd like to cover are the differences between niche and authority style websites as well as the pros and cons of each.

Want to read the rest of the book?

It is available here:

http://www.amazon.com/How-Make-Money-Amazon-Associate-ebook

More Books by Chris Guthrie

Buying Websites – How to Invest in Online Real Estate

How To Make Your First $1,000 With Online Surveys

www.ingramcontent.com/pod-product-compliance
Lightning Source LLC
Chambersburg PA
CBHW071820170526
45167CB00003B/1377